Society of Snow

The True Story of Flight 571 and Miracle of the Andes

Harper Blackwood

Copyright

Disclaimer

This nonfiction book chronicles the events surrounding the 1972 crash of Uruguayan Air Force Flight 571 and the subsequent survival of its passengers. While every attempt has been taken to authentically reflect the events, experiences, and viewpoints of the survivors, it is important to note that people's memories of terrible situations differ. The narratives contained in this book are based on extensive interviews, research, and available historical data; yet, some facts may be modified by time, personal perception of events, and the difficulties that come with recalling intense situations.

The book discusses serious issues, such as survival cannibalism, which may be upsetting to some readers. These subjects are presented with great respect for individuals affected and are included to provide a thorough understanding of the survivors' experiences.

The legal, ethical, and moral discussions in this book do not seek to provide definite solutions or verdicts. They were included to explore the complicated issues that occurred as a result of the survivors' unusual circumstances. Readers are invited to approach these themes with a fresh perspective and to contemplate the enormous influence that such experiences can have on people.

Names, locations, and events have been portrayed as accurately as feasible, but some minor details may have been changed to improve clarity or protect the privacy of persons concerned. This book is intended to recognize the survivors' fortitude, perseverance, and humanity while also providing insight into the psychological, emotional, and physical problems they faced.

The author and publisher of this book do not condone or support any of the behaviors depicted in the story. The book is both a historical record and a reflection on the severe conditions that forced remarkable decisions in order to survive. Readers should analyze the context in which these decisions were taken, and approach the content with empathy and understanding.

Table of Contents

Introduction

On October 13, 1972, a Uruguayan Air Force Fairchild FH-227D aircraft took off from Montevideo, Uruguay, carrying 45 passengers and crew members, the majority of them were teenage members of the Old Christians Club rugby team, heading for Santiago, Chile. The flight was supposed to be a short, exciting excursion for the team, packed with camaraderie and the prospect of a friendly encounter. Instead, it set the stage for one of modern history's most incredible and harrowing survival stories.

When the jet crashed into the rugged and inhospitable Andes Mountains, the lives of everyone on board were shattered in an instant.

The initial impact killed twelve passengers, and when the survivors emerged from the wreckage, they found themselves in a terrible scenario: stranded in a bleak, freezing wilderness thousands of feet above sea level, with no sign of aid on the horizon. Over the next 72 days, these survivors would face unprecedented adversity, including the elements, malnutrition, injury, and the psychological toll of the event.

The narrative of Flight 571 is more than just one of survival against all odds; it is a very human story about the limits of endurance, the power of the human spirit, and the ethical quandaries that arise when life and death are at stake. It is a story that questions our notion of morality and the lengths we will go to be confronted with the harsh reality of our own mortality.

This book transports you to the heart of the Andes, providing an in-depth look at the events that occurred over the course of 72 days, as described by the survivors. Through their eyes, we will witness the terror of the crash, the agony of starving, the desperate decisions made in the face of death, and the eventual triumph of the human will to survive.

However, this story is about more than just surviving; it is about the aftermath—the psychological scars, the fight to return to normalcy, and the terrible impact these events had on the survivors and their families. It's about the media frenzy that followed their rescue, the ongoing ethical issues, and how this incredible story has been remembered, recreated, and reinterpreted throughout time.

As you read this book, you will be confronted with questions that cannot be easily answered. What exactly does it mean to survive? What would you do in the most severe situations? How do we reconcile our acts with our values when the rules of civilization are no longer applicable? These are the questions that the Flight 571 survivors had to answer, and they are questions that we can all relate to.

The story of Flight 571 exemplifies the human spirit's tenacity, community strength, and unwavering determination to live. It's a story that will move, challenge, and stay with you long after you've turned the last page.

Chapter One

The Ill-Fated Flight

The Old Christians Club, Uruguay's rugby squad, has a story of brotherhood, youthful enthusiasm, and ambitions of victory. These young guys, many of whom were in their late teens and early twenties, were united not just by their love of the sport, but also by deep friendships formed over years of playing together. They were a close-knit bunch, backed up by a few friends and family members who had joined them on what was supposed to be a brief and thrilling trip to Chile. They had no idea that their journey would turn out to be a terrifying odyssey that would put their bonds, resilience, and desire to survive to the test in the most harsh conditions possible.

The team flew aboard a Fairchild FH-227D, a twin-engine turboprop that had been in service for a few years. This aircraft was well-known for its dependability, and it was frequently utilized on regional flights across South America. Colonel Julio Ferradas, an experienced and well recognized aviator, flew the plane with Lieutenant-Colonel Dante Lagurara as his co-pilot. The aircraft was designed to handle the flight's altitude and the rough terrain of the Andes, a trip that many planes had flown without incident.

On October 12, 1972, the squad and its supporters assembled at Montevideo's Carrasco International Airport. They were upbeat as they boarded the Fairchild, looking forward to the impending match in Santiago, Chile. The departure was regular, and the flight plan was designed to ensure a safe travel across the Andes Mountains. However, due to poor weather, the flight was delayed, and the team spent the night in Mendoza, Argentina, before continuing their journey the next day.

The following morning, on October 13, the plane took off again, with everyone on board eager to get to their destination. The weather was still not ideal, with low clouds covering the Andean peaks, but the pilots were confident in their ability to manage the path. As they approached the Alps, the flight plan required them to fly via a tight corridor between the high peaks, which needed precision navigation.

Unfortunately, as the aircraft approached its final landing in Chile, a crucial navigational error occurred. The pilots thought they'd cleared the Andes and started descending, unaware that they were still deep within the mountain range. This error was exacerbated by the inclement weather, which made visual confirmation of their location practically impossible. The plane was considerably further east than the pilots thought, and as they dropped, they were heading directly for the mountains.

The Fairchild was stuck in a downdraft, and the pilots quickly recognized their mistake. The mountains loomed ahead, and despite their best efforts to get up, it was too late. The airplane collided with the peak, tearing off a part of the right wing. The jet lost control and crashed into the mountainside, breaking apart as it skidded across the snow-covered ground.

The impact was severe. The fuselage separated into many parts, sending wreckage and passengers across the mountainside. Those who survived the original catastrophe were stunned and injured, unable to realize what had occurred. The crash's loudness was replaced by an eerie calm, interrupted only by the moans of the injured and the howling wind that ripped through the mountains.

At that moment, the team's journey had transformed from a hopeful excursion to a perilous struggle for survival. The navigational error had sealed their destiny, putting them in one of the most distant and hostile settings on

Earth. The Fairchild FH-227D, which had previously served as their mode of transportation to a friendly match, was now nothing more than a destroyed shell in the snow, surrounded by the Andes' vast and brutal scenery.

The survivors, many of whom suffered shattered bones, major cuts, and other injuries, were confronted with the awful reality of their position. They were far from civilization and had no imminent possibility of being rescued. The choice to descend too soon had cost lives and put the remaining passengers through an awful trauma. The squad, which had been so full of life just hours before, now needed all of their power and solidarity to survive in the face of overwhelming odds.

This marked the start of their perilous trip, which would put them to the test in ways they could never have anticipated. The rugby squad, once linked by their love of the game, was now bound together by their struggle for survival, with each member playing an important part in the days and weeks that followed. Their narrative would go down as one of the most astonishing accounts of human perseverance and the determination to endure in the face of adversity.

Chapter Two

The Crash

The impact of the crash was sudden and severe. On October 13, 1972, Flight 571 collided with the Andes Mountains while carrying 45 people, including members of the Old Christians Club rugby team. The aircraft, a Fairchild FH-227D, had been on a course that was supposed to carry it safely over the high peaks, but a navigational error caused calamity. As the plane fell prematurely, it collided with the pinnacle of a mountain, ripping off its right wing and sending it into a catastrophic spiral. Within seconds, the fuselage collided with the mountainside, shattering apart as it skidded across the snow-covered ground.

For the passengers inside, the crash was a scary whirl of noise and movement. Nando Parrado, one of the rugby players, later described the terrifying feeling of being slammed against the side of the airplane as it disintegrated. His mother, Eugenia Parrado, and sister, Susana Parrado, sat beside him. Eugenia died quickly in the incident, while Susana was badly injured. Nando was struck unconscious, only to awaken hours later to the biting cold and the bleak reality around him.

Roberto Canessa, another team member and medical student, also survived the hit. Despite his own injuries, he swiftly assumed the responsibility of tending to the wounded. He moved from one survivor to another, doing the best he could with his scant medical expertise. With no supplies and only the most basic equipment at his disposal, Canessa was able to stabilize some of the injured, including Fernando

"Nando" Parrado, who had sustained a severe head injury.

The immediate aftermath of the incident was chaotic. The survivors, many of whom were hurt and disoriented, attempted to understand what had occurred. The terrain around them was bleak, freezing tundra, a far cry from the lush green pastures they'd left behind. The cold was persistent, penetrating through tattered garments and biting into bare skin. The survivors understood they needed to move swiftly if they were to survive, but the shock of the accident made it difficult to concentrate.

Canessa's close friend and fellow rugby player, Antonio "Tintín" Vizintín, was among the first to recognize the severity of the situation. He started organizing the survivors, helping to extract individuals from the wreckage and gathering any supplies they could find. Vizintín's fast thinking and leadership were critical in the early hours, when the survivors struggled to fashion a temporary shelter from the fuselage pieces.

As the survivors appraised their circumstances, the true tragedy of what had occurred became clear. Of the 45 persons on board, 12 died instantaneously in the disaster, including Nando Parrado's mother, Eugenia, and numerous teammates. Another five would die within hours from their injuries and the cold. Among the injured, the situation was terrible. Nando's sister, Susana Parrado, lay unconscious and severely hurt. Despite Canessa's best efforts, he realized there was little he could do to save her.

The survivors were forced to face the harsh reality of their circumstances. They were imprisoned in one of the world's most remote and unforgiving settings, miles from civilization and unable to phone for aid. The plane's radio had been destroyed in the crash, so they had no method of signaling their whereabouts. They had only a few chocolate bars, a handful of nuts, and a few bottles of wine left. It was obvious that these provisions would not last long.

As night fell, they began to realize the brutal reality of their situation. The temperature plunged, and the survivors huddled together for warmth, using the plane's shredded seats and debris as temporary insulation. The cold was severe, and without adequate clothing or shelter, the risk of hypothermia was considerable. The survivors understood that their chances of survival were minimal unless they were rescued quickly. However, as the days passed and no rescue arrived, hope began to fade.

On the second day after the collision, the survivors met to debate their options. After regaining consciousness, Nando Parrado, Roberto Canessa, and Antonio Vizintín led the debate. They realized they needed to ration their meager food supply and arrange their resources if they were to survive. During this meeting, they first considered the prospect of having to go out into the mountains in search of help. The concept was terrible, but the alternative—waiting to die—was unimaginable.

Over the next few days, the survivors had to confront the harsh truth of their circumstances. Nando's sister, Susana Parrado, died from her injuries, dealing a heartbreaking blow to her brother, who had already lost his mother. More survivors became weakened as their bodies struggled to deal with the cold and a lack of nourishment. The situation became increasingly desperate, and the survivors realized that they would have to take severe steps to stay alive.

As time passed, the survivors of Flight 571 faced unprecedented trials. The tough Andean environment, with its frigid temperatures and dangerous terrain, was unrelenting. However, despite the overwhelming odds, they refused to give up. They fought for survival with courage, cunning, and unrelenting tenacity, even as hope for rescue faded into the freezing expanse of the mountains.

This was the start of their extraordinary journey, which would test them to the boundaries of human endurance and leave a lasting legacy of perseverance and optimism in the face of the most frightening hardship.

Chapter Three

The Struggle for Survival

The days following the disaster of Flight 571 were marked by a sobering realization: the survivors were stranded in an environment that provided nothing to maintain life. As the horror of the collision subsided, the harsh truth of their predicament became clear, and the survivors faced one of their most pressing challenges: inadequate resources. Food and water, both vital for survival, were in low supply.

The limited rations recovered from the debris comprised a few chocolate bars, snacks, and a little amount of alcohol. The survivors understood that these resources would not last long, especially with 27 people to feed. Roberto Canessa, whose medical degree gave him a scientific viewpoint, estimated the calories they could get from their restricted food supply and concluded that rationing was their only alternative. Each person was given only a small amount of chocolate or a taste of wine every day, barely enough to fight off hunger, let alone offer the energy required to survive in such difficult conditions.

Water was another essential concern. The cold, dry air of the Andes provided little moisture, thus the survivors quickly became dehydrated. With no streams or natural water sources nearby, they were obliged to melt snow on the fuselage's aluminum panels, a laborious and labor-intensive process. However, even this provided only modest amounts of water, and the extreme cold caused the snowmelt to freeze practically as soon as it was created. Each drop was valuable, and the survivors rationed it carefully, knowing that without water, their condition would worsen.

As the days passed, the survivors began to feel the effects of a lack of food. Hunger gnawed at them relentlessly, weakening both their bodies and brains. The cold intensified their agony. At an elevation of more than 12,000 feet, the temperature dropped dramatically at night, frequently falling well below freezing. The survivors lacked adequate clothing and shelter to protect themselves from the elements. They crowded close within the fuselage, wrapping themselves in whatever fabric remnants they could find to stay warm. Despite their attempts, the cold persisted, seeping into their bones and draining their strength.

For Nando Parrado, Roberto Canessa, and the others, the cold was both a physical and mental enemy. The freezing conditions made every movement and task agonizing. Simple tasks such as melting snow or moving garbage required enormous effort, and the risk of frostbite was constant. Some survivors experienced numbness and tingling in their extremities, which were early indicators of frostbite and would intensify over time. The cold also made sleep difficult, with survivors frequently waking up shivering violently, unable to generate enough heat to keep them warm.

Injuries sustained during the incident exacerbated the group's hardships. Many survivors suffered fractured bones, major lacerations, and internal damage. Roberto Canessa tried his hardest to treat them, but with no medical supplies and very minimal expertise, his options were restricted. He and the other survivors had to improvise, using wreckage to splint shattered limbs and ripped garments to heal wounds. Infections were a persistent threat, as dirt and debris from the accident site infected open wounds. Even minor injuries could be fatal if not treated with antibiotics and proper medical treatment.

Nando Parrado, who had suffered a severe brain injury in the incident, struggled with excruciating migraines and dizziness, but he pushed himself to stay active and help wherever he could. Their condition had a significant psychological influence on everyone. The realization that they were far from aid, combined with the physical suffering they were experiencing, caused a sense of hopelessness that was difficult to overcome. Despite this, the survivors understood they couldn't afford to give up. Every day was a battle not just against the physical elements, but also against the looming sense of hopelessness that threatened to overtake them.

In this perilous scenario, leadership and decision-making became critical for the group's survival. While many people were killed in the disaster, including their coach and numerous experienced adults, the survivors rapidly recognized that they needed to organize themselves if they were to survive the catastrophe. Nando Parrado, despite his ailments, emerged as an important character in this process. His innate leadership abilities, along with his resolve to live, made him a focal point for the group.

Roberto Canessa, with his medical knowledge and calm manner, also played an important role. Parrado and Canessa, along with other survivors like Antonio "Tintín" Vizintín and Gustavo Zerbino, began making difficult decisions to shape their fight for survival. They devised a system for rationing food and water, formed search parties to look for new supplies, and established guidelines for energy conservation and remaining warm. These decisions were rarely simple, and they frequently forced the survivors to face difficult truths about their predicament.

One of the most difficult decisions they had to make was realizing that in order to survive, they would have to explore options that would normally be unimaginable. As the days grew into weeks and their food supply deteriorated, the survivors were forced to consider cannibalism. It was a desperate choice made after all other possibilities had been exhausted. After much deliberation and hesitation, they determined that the bodies of those who had perished could give the food they required to survive. This difficult decision was made collaboratively, with each survivor carefully considering the moral and ethical ramifications before agreeing to it.

Parrado, Canessa, and others provided critical leadership in keeping the group on track and cohesive. They recognized the importance of maintaining a sense of order and purpose, not just for physical survival but also for mental health. The group created routines, with each survivor assigned specific responsibilities, such as gathering snow to melt for water, caring for the injured, or keeping an eye out for potential rescuers. These rituals provided them with a sense of control over their position, no matter how tenuous, and helped to prevent feelings of helplessness from taking hold.

As the survivors battled the environment, injuries, and a lack of food and water, they had to rely on one another in ways they never expected. The relationships built through shared tragedy were a source of strength, allowing them to face the unthinkable. Leadership, both formal and informal, was crucial in this process, guiding the group through the complex and often unpleasant decisions that needed to be made.

Finally, the survivors were able to persist thanks to their inventiveness, determination, and good leadership. Despite their dreadful position and insurmountable trials, they never gave up hope. They fought for survival together, drawing on their inner reserves of strength and fortitude and supporting one another during the most difficult times of their ordeal. Flight 571's narrative is more than just one of calamity; it is also one of human endurance, the strength of collective action, and the determination to endure in the face of overwhelming odds.

Chapter Four

The Moral Dilemma

As the days went into weeks, the survivors of Flight 571 faced a worsening predicament. Stranded in the frigid wilderness of the Andes, their scant food supplies had long since run out. Hunger, which had begun as a gnawing pain, quickly became an all-consuming anguish. When the human body is deprived of food, it begins to break down its own tissues for energy, resulting in weakness, bewilderment, and an indescribable sense of despair. For the surviving, the reality of famine became brutally clear.

Nando Parrado, Roberto Canessa, and the others had done everything possible to ration the food they had recovered from the debris. Despite their greatest efforts, it simply wasn't enough. The chocolate, crackers, and wine that had been their lifeline at the beginning were gone, leaving the survivors with just snow and ice. The cold stole their vitality, and each day was a battle to find the energy to keep going. Their bodies, once muscular and athletic, were deteriorating, and the chance of rescue appeared increasingly far.

As famine set in, the survivors began to consider an unimaginable yet essential decision. With no alternative food sources accessible, they were confronted with the harsh truth that the only thing left to eat were the bodies of those killed in the accident. Cannibalism horrified them because it contradicted every moral and ethical standard they knew. But the alternative—slowly starving to death—was also unfathomable.

The choice to resort to cannibalism was not taken lightly. It was born of pure desperation, a decision made after all other options had been explored. In the days preceding the decision, the survivors had heated debates regarding the ethical ramifications of what they were planning. These discussions were laden with emotion, as each participant struggled with their own convictions and the tragedy of what they were forced to consider.

Roberto Canessa, a medical student before the crash, was a significant figure in these talks. He highlighted the basic importance of taking protein to keep their bodies from shutting down completely. He also framed the decision in terms of survival, claiming that those who died in the disaster would have wanted the survivors to go to any length to live. Nando Parrado, who had already lost his mother and sister, fought with the concept but eventually accepted that there was no other option. The group struck an agreement, albeit a hesitant and unpleasant one.

The survivors tackled their work with grave reverence. They were aware that what they were doing would haunt them for the rest of their lives, but they also realized that it was the only way to survive. They took great care to be as courteous as possible, reciting prayers and seeking forgiveness before ingesting the flesh of their deceased companions. The situation was highly traumatic, and each survivor dealt with it in their own unique way. Some sought to disconnect emotionally, viewing it as a necessary but unpleasant chore. Others were overwhelmed with remorse and grief, unable to reconcile the conduct with their moral views.

The psychological toll of the choice was enormous. Even though the survivors understood cognitively that they had no option, the emotional toll was severe. Many of them felt extreme guilt, shame, and a profound sense of loss. They were grieving not only the deaths of their companions, but also the loss of their own innocence and humanity. The act of cannibalism, while necessary, left significant psychological wounds that took years to heal.

In the days and weeks that followed, the survivors tried to cope with the consequences of their decision. They continued to limit their food, always aware of the need to stretch it as far as possible. However, the psychological impacts proved more difficult to handle. Nightmares, memories, and despair were widespread as the survivors battled to accept their actions. They sought consolation in each other, openly discussing their experiences and attempting to encourage one another throughout the worst times.

The survivors' decision to resort to cannibalism marked a turning point in their journey. It was the moment they realized how isolated they were and how far they would have to go to survive. It was a decision that would permanently alter their lives. However, it was also a life-saving decision, allowing them to survive until they were rescued.

The narrative of Flight 571 demonstrates the human spirit's resilience and will to endure, even in the face of incredible adversity. The survivors' decision to resort to cannibalism was not made lightly, but rather as a group. It was an unavoidable decision that put their morality, ethics, and humanity to the test. However, it was a decision that ultimately saved their lives, allowing them to return home and share their experience with the rest of the world.

Chapter Five

Search and Rescue Attempts

When news broke on October 13, 1972, that Flight 571 had gone missing over the Andes Mountains, the passengers' families were left in shock and dismay. The plane, carrying 45 people, including members of the Old Christians Club rugby team, went missing during what was intended to be a normal journey from Montevideo, Uruguay, to Santiago, Chile. The rugby players, many of whom were in their late teens and early twenties, were cherished sons, brothers, and friends, and the prospect of their becoming lost in the hazardous mountains was agonizing for those who hoped for their safe return.

As the hours passed without any word from the airplane, family gathered at Carrasco International Airport, hoping and praying for a miracle. The initial confusion gave way to a hasty search for information. On October 14, just one day after the disaster, Uruguayan authorities and the Chilean military initiated a search mission. Aircraft were deployed to explore the route that Flight 571 was meant to travel, with pilots staring down at the huge, snow-covered Andes for any signs of the missing airliner.

Those early days saw extensive search attempts. The pilots flying over the Andes encountered severe challenges: dense cloud cover, strong winds, and rocky, impassable terrain made it nearly difficult to see anything on the ground.

The Andes' peaks, some of the highest in the world, reached 22,000 feet, and the plane's wreckage was hidden in a lonely valley at a height of around 12,000 feet. Despite their best efforts, the search teams discovered nothing. Each day that went without finding the debris felt like another step closer to losing hope.

As the search continued into the third day, October 16, 1972, the families of the passengers became increasingly concerned. Every phone call and update from the authorities sparked a mixture of hope and fear. The media coverage heightened the suspense, with reporters guessing on the fate of the jet and its occupants. The families, caught between hope and misery, could only wait and pray.

Despite the continuous search, efforts to find the wreckage were useless. The search teams scoured hundreds of square miles, but the vastness of the Andes and the limitations of technology at the time made it unlikely that they would find the debris. The plane's white fuselage blended almost seamlessly with the snow-covered mountains, rendering it practically invisible from above.

By October 20, 1972, a week after the incident, the situation had deteriorated. The authorities had to consider the potential that the plane had crashed in such a distant and inaccessible location that it would never be discovered. The difficult circumstances and lack of sightings prompted debates about the practicality of continuing the search. The relatives, who had hoped for a rescue, began to fear the worst.

Finally, on October 21, 1972, after nine days of searching, Uruguayan and Chilean authorities made the heartbreaking decision to discontinue the search. The announcement was heartbreaking to the family. It seemed as if their loved ones had received a death sentence. Many people found the news too hard to stomach. They had hoped that their sons, siblings, and friends were still alive and waiting to be rescued. That hope was dashed now that the quest had come to an end. The grief was profound, leaving many in shock and amazement.

The survivors of Flight 571 in the distant Andes were unaware that the search had been called off. For days, they'd heard the distant hum of airplane engines and urgently sought to announce their existence. When they heard a plane, they hurried to wave bright objects or mirrors, hoping against hope that they would be noticed. But as the days passed and the planes became less frequent, the survivors realized the dreadful truth: no one was coming for them.

By October 24, 1972, more than ten days after the disaster, the survivors had come to the harsh realization that they were indeed alone. Nando Parrado and Roberto Canessa, who had emerged as the group's leaders, reviewed the problem with the other members. They realized that their sole hope of survival now depended on their capacity to seek help. Staying put and awaiting rescue was no longer an option. They would have to take action for themselves.

The choice to go out into the mountains in quest of help was not taken lightly. Hunger, cold, and the stress of the crash had left the survivors weak. But they knew they couldn't last much longer in their current situation. On October 26, 1972, Parrado, Canessa, and Antonio Vizintín began preparing for a challenging journey across the Andes. They were aware that the trek would be risky, but they also understood that it was their last chance of survival.

The revelation that they were alone, with no one to rescue them, was a watershed moment for the survivors. It represented the start of a new phase in their struggle—one in which they would take control of their own fate. Parrado, Canessa, and the others' tenacity and fortitude propelled them to safety. They recognized the immensity of the task ahead, but they also realized they had no other option.

The choice to leave the mountains was a combination of desperation and exceptional bravery. It was a decision that ultimately resulted in their rescue and safety. But in those dark days of late October 1972, it was a decision based on the stark fact that they were alone in one of the most hostile environments on the planet, and that their only salvation lay in their own hands.

Chapter Six

The Expedition for Help

As the survivors of Flight 571 understood there would be no rescue, their only hope for life lay in their own hands. By late November 1972, more than a month after the catastrophe, the need for assistance had grown acute. The gang recognized that staying at the crash site meant likely death due to malnutrition and exposure. The only alternative left was to undertake a trip over the harsh Andes to reach civilization.

The decision to undertake this risky voyage was not taken lightly. The survivors realized the journey would be extremely perilous, so they had to carefully pick who would undertake it. Those picked had to be in peak physical condition, despite the effects of malnutrition, cold, and injuries. After deliberation, Nando Parrado, Roberto Canessa, and Antonio "Tintín" Vizintín agreed to travel. Parrado, who had demonstrated incredible resilience and leadership throughout the ordeal, was resolved to seek assistance. Canessa, with his medical training, understood the stakes better than anybody else and realized that each day they waited would diminish their chances of life. Vizintín, a strong and dependable character, was picked for his perseverance and courage to face the unknown.

The strategy was precise. They gathered what little supplies they had left, which included fragments of the plane's insulation to guard against the cold, some makeshift sleeping bags, and strips of leather from the jet seats that they thought would serve as nourishment along the way. On December 12, 1972, Parrado, Canessa, and Vizintín embarked on their adventure after saying goodbye to their fellow survivors who remained at the wreckage. The weight of their task was great on their shoulders; they were their own and their companions' last hope.

The trip across the Andes was nothing short of a nightmare. The environment was dangerous, with steep cliffs, deep snow, and bitter gusts that ripped through their homemade garments. Each step was taxing, and the thin air at high elevation made breathing difficult. The guys had already been debilitated by weeks of fasting, so every ounce of energy needed to be preserved. Despite facing hardships, Parrado, Canessa, and Vizintín remained determined to reach civilization and ensure their survival.

Vizintín was sent back to the crash site with some supplies after a three-day hike that proved more arduous than expected. The group feared they would not have enough resources to complete the expedition. Parrado and Canessa went on, reaching even higher altitudes in search of a path out of the mountains. On December 20, 1972, after nine days of unrelenting labor, they glimpsed something incredible: a twisting river, indicating that they were approaching lower heights and, possibly, civilization.

As they followed the river downstream, their hopes began to grow. On December 21, 1972, they spotted a man on horseback in the distance.

Sergio Catalán was a Chilean shepherd. Despite the language barrier, the severity of their predicament was obvious. Parrado and Canessa desperately attempted to convey their critical need for assistance. Catalán, stunned by their presence and realizing that something awful had occurred, stated that he would come the next day with assistance. Catalán kept his promise the next morning, bringing supplies and informing authorities about the two survivors and the others who remained stranded in the mountains.

On December 22, 1972, the world learned that there were survivors from Flight 571. The Chilean military promptly launched a rescue operation. Helicopters were sent to the crash site, led by Canessa and Parrado. The trek to safety for the remaining survivors began that day, when rescuers arrived at the accident site and discovered 14 more survivors who had spent nearly 70 days in the mountains. The conditions were so bad that helicopters could only transport half of the survivors on the first day, with the rest rescued the next day, December 23, 1972.

For the survivors, the arrival of the rescuers represented both relief and the end of a horrible chapter in their lives. They were taken to hospitals in Santiago and treated for starvation, frostbite, and other injuries incurred during their adventure. The world watched in astonishment as their survival story unfolded—one of tremendous hardship, resilience, and the tenacious human spirit. Nando Parrado and Roberto Canessa were recognized as heroes, not just for their courage in making the journey, but also for their commitment to save their comrades.

The trek from the Andes to safety marked the end of an epic effort. The survivors of Flight 571 had seen the worst that nature could hurl at them, yet they had endured. Their rescue represented the conclusion of an odyssey that had tested their human fortitude to its limits, as well as a return to a world that had almost given them up for lost. Their narrative is still one of the most incredible tales of survival in contemporary history, demonstrating the power of hope, determination, and the desire to survive.

Chapter Seven

Rescue and Recovery

On December 22, 1972, a rescue attempt to save the remaining survivors of Flight 571 began. Following Nando Parrado and Roberto Canessa's remarkable journey over the Andes and their encounter with the Chilean shepherd, Sergio Catalán, word quickly spread to the authorities. The Chilean military, sensing the gravity of the situation, swiftly planned a helicopter evacuation expedition. The weather remained difficult, with snow and strong winds making the operation dangerous. However, the rescuers were determined to reach the crash site and save the 14 survivors who had spent more than two months in the highlands.

Two Bell UH-1 helicopters were despatched from San Fernando, Chile, carrying rescue teams of paramedics, soldiers, and mountain guides experienced with the tough terrain. The helicopters had to navigate through small valleys and over steep Andean peaks, which presented various obstacles. The helicopters struggled to sustain lift due to the high altitude and thin air, and the landing zone near the crash scene was dangerous, surrounded by steep cliffs and deep snow.

When the helicopters arrived at the crash site, rescuers were faced with a surprising and heartbreaking scene. The surviving, gaunt and frail, were barely recognisable as the robust young athletes they once were. Despite their desperate situation, the survivors were happy to meet the rescuers. The first set of survivors was evacuated that day, with helicopters limited to carrying only seven people at a time due to altitude and weight limits. The remaining seven survivors were left with rescuers to wait for a second flight, which arrived the next day, December 23, 1972.

The evacuation was a physical and emotional hardship. The survivors, some of whom could scarcely walk, were carefully loaded onto helicopters and transported out of the Andes, leaving behind the crash site, which had served as both their home and prison for 72 days. As the helicopters lifted from the disaster scene, transporting the survivors to safety, those who survived felt a great sense of relief. They were finally on the way home.

The surviving were taken to hospitals in Santiago, where medical personnel were ready to treat them for acute starvation, frostbite, and other afflictions. As word of their rescue spread, their relatives, who had feared the worst, learned that their loved ones were alive. The emotional reunions that ensued were tremendous, bringing tears of pleasure and relief. For many families, learning that their sons, siblings, and friends had survived felt like a miracle, especially since the search had been called off weeks earlier.

At the hospital, the survivors were greeted by a slew of physicians, nurses, and officials, but the most moving moments occurred when they were finally reunited with their families. Parents embraced their boys, moved with emotion at seeing them alive, albeit emaciated and fragile. After facing such tremendous pain, the survivors clung to their loved ones for solace. The reunions were bittersweet, as survivors were reminded of those who had died in the mountains.

For the families, the return of their loved ones was a time of tremendous thankfulness, as well as reflection on the loss they had experienced. The joy of the reunion was tempered by mourning for those who had died in the crash, and for the survivors, the comfort of returning home was weighed against the weight of their harrowing experiences in the Andes.

The rescue story rapidly became a global phenomenon. The media, which had followed

Flight 571's disappearance and subsequent search attempts, converged to Santiago to chronicle the 16 young men's amazing survival. Reporters from all around the world flocked at the survivors' hospitals and homes, ready to relate their stories of what had transpired in the mountains.

The survivors, who had been forced into the spotlight, were now the subject of intense media investigation. Their story of survival, the horrible situations they faced, and the difficult decisions they had to make, including the necessity of cannibalism, enthralled the globe. The details of their tragedy frightened and captivated the public, and the survivors were forced to manage the complicated emotions that came with sharing their story with a worldwide audience.

Interviews, news conferences, and media appearances became regular occurrences for the survivors. They were frequently prompted to describe their experiences, experiencing the anguish while attempting to explain what had happened. The media frenzy generated both support and criticism. While many commended the survivors for their bravery and tenacity, others were uneasy about the harsh reality of their survival, notably their decision to resort to cannibalism.

Despite the difficulties of dealing with the media, the survivors remained united, encouraging one another as they adjusted to life after their trauma. Flight 571 became one of the most fascinating survival stories of the twentieth century, serving as a strong monument to the human spirit's tenacity.

While the survivors were rescued and reunited with their families, the remains of those killed in the crash remained on the mountain. The decision to leave the deceased behind was terrible, but it was necessary during the evacuation. The crash site's remote and dangerous location made recovering the bodies a daunting challenge.

After the survivors were successfully evacuated in early January 1973, a recovery expedition was undertaken to rescue the bodies of those who died. The Chilean military, along with forensic scientists and mountain guides, carried out the task. The team encountered the same dangers that had beset the rescue operation: extreme cold, high altitude, and challenging terrain. It was a melancholy process, as rescuers painstakingly recovered the corpses of the passengers who had died in the crash or during the subsequent agony.

The bodies were subsequently returned to their family in Uruguay, where they were appropriately buried. The survivors, terribly saddened by the loss of their friends and teammates, attended the funerals to pay their final respects to those who did not make it out of the Andes. The retrieval of the deceased provided a sense of closure for the families and survivors, but it also highlighted the great loss that had occurred.

The survivors marked the site of the crash, high in the Andes, with a modest cross as a monument to those who died. It is still a site of reflection and recollection, a clear reminder of the tragedy and the extraordinary story of survival that unfolded. The bodies left behind were finally buried, but the memory of their lives, as well as the horrible struggle that the survivors faced, would live on in the minds of all who were touched by the narrative of Flight 571.

Chapter Eight

The Aftermath

The spectacular rescue of Flight 571 survivors in December 1972 sparked a global media phenomenon. The tragic accounts of their 72-day journey in the Andes, along with the unexpected revelation of their desperate recourse to cannibalism, piqued the interest of news outlets worldwide. The media's interest in the tale was palpable, and it quickly led to a flood of sensationalist coverage that frequently stressed stunning headlines over the survivors' compassion.

Journalists from all over the world raced to Santiago and Montevideo, hungry for exclusive interviews and images. The survivors, who were still physically and mentally frail after their tragedy, were thrown into the spotlight. Reporters peppered them with questions, frequently focusing on the most spectacular aspects of their story—how they had survived by devouring the remains of their slain colleagues and teammates. Headlines were dramatic, stressing horrific details in ways that enthralled and scared the audience. Newspapers and magazines all over the world published stories with names like "Cannibalism in the Andes" and "Survival at All Costs," which, while selling papers, also oversimplified and sensationalized the survivors' experiences.

The survivors saw the increasing public scrutiny as a mixed benefit. While it allowed them to share their experience with a global audience, it also required them to relive the pain of their ordeal on multiple occasions. The media's focus on cannibalism, in particular, overshadowed other aspects of their story, such as their extraordinary physical and mental endurance, community strength, and emerging leadership. The continuous questioning, as well as the public's obsession with the more morbid aspects of their survival, took their toll on the survivors, many of whom struggled to cope with the unexpected and overwhelming attention.

The public's reaction to the survivors' account was very split. On the one hand, they were widely admired for their fortitude and determination. Many people around the world were touched by the survivors' bravery and sheer resolve, which kept them alive in such harsh conditions. These supporters sent letters, presents, and notes of solidarity, expressing their amazement at what the survivors had gone through and their thankfulness for their rescue.

On the other hand, the discovery that the survivors had turned to cannibalism provoked widespread outrage. While some people recognized that the survivors had been forced to make an impossible decision, others were greatly upset by the idea and questioned the morality of their acts. Some criticized the survivors, questioning if their actions could ever be acceptable under such grave circumstances. This judgment added another layer of anguish to their experience, forcing them to defend actions performed under the most desperate of circumstances.

The controversy surrounding the survivors' conduct sparked heated legal and ethical arguments, especially in Uruguay and Chile. Legal experts were consulted to determine whether the survivors would face any legal consequences for their acts. Finally, it was agreed that the survivors acted out of necessity, and that their decision to engage in cannibalism was a question of survival rather than a criminal act. The court system recognized the terrible circumstances they had encountered and concluded that they could not be judged using the same standards as those in ordinary circumstances.

However, the ethical disputes were much more intricate and lasted for years. Philosophers, theologians, and ethicists discussed the moral implications of the survivors' decision. Was it morally appropriate to adopt such harsh steps for the sake of survival? Did the circumstances they encountered free them of moral responsibility? These debates emphasized the challenging and often uncomfortable concerns that occur when humans are tested to their limits. While some maintained that the survivors did what was necessary to stay alive, others questioned the moral and ethical consequences of their conduct.

As the survivors began to share their own stories, it became evident that everyone had experienced the trauma in a unique way. Nando Parrado, for example, spoke frankly about his deep grief after losing his mother and sister in the tragedy. His choice to start on the perilous journey over the Andes to seek assistance was motivated not just by a wish to survive, but also by a desire to honor the memories of his loved ones. Parrado's narrative of the journey, which he took with Roberto Canessa, became one of the story's most riveting elements, demonstrating both the physical hardships they experienced and the inner power that kept them going.

Before the catastrophe, Roberto Canessa, a medical student, provided insights on the group's psychological and ethical difficulties. He discussed the decisions they made, including the tough decision to consume their departed friends' bodies, and how they rationalized these choices to themselves and each other. Canessa's views on the tragedy emphasized the survivors' strong relationships, as well as the mental and emotional toll the incident had placed on them.

Other survivors provided their own viewpoints, each adding fresh layers to the story. Some concentrated on the daily battle to stay warm, get water, and remain hopeful in the face of crushing despair. Others discussed the role of leadership within the group and how they had worked together to make difficult decisions. These individual testimonies provided a more nuanced perspective of what had happened in the mountains, demonstrating that the story was about more than just survival; it was also about the complicated human emotions and connections that had kept them going.

All of the survivors suffered significant psychological trauma as a result of the encounter. Many of them suffered from nightmares, flashbacks, and feelings of guilt and shame. The decision to practice cannibalism, while vital for survival, caused significant emotional wounds. Some survivors struggled to reconcile their conduct with their moral values, and the public scrutiny only exacerbated these feelings. Sharing their stories, both with the media and with their families, was a double-edged sword—while it helped some survivors come to terms with their experiences, it also forced them to confront the trauma in terrible ways.

In the years since, the Flight 571 story has been memorialized in books, documentaries, and films. The survivors collaborated with journalists and authors to ensure that their narrative was portrayed correctly and with the necessary detail. The most well-known of these works is "Alive," a book by Piers Paul Read released in 1974 that became an international bestseller and was later turned into a successful movie in 1993. The book and film expanded the story's reach, cementing it as one of the most miraculous survival stories in history.

The survivors of Flight 571 soon became powerful voices in their own right, sharing their stories through public speaking engagements and interviews, as well as offering insights into what it means to survive in the face of enormous hardship. Their narrative continues to resonate with people all across the world, not only because of the harrowing circumstances they faced, but also because it raises important questions about human nature, morality, and the will to live. The memory of their ordeal is a monument to the human spirit's tenacity, as well as a lesson that hope and courage may triumph even in the most difficult circumstances.

www.ingramcontent.com/pod-product-compliance
Ingram Content Group UK Ltd.
Pitfield, Milton Keynes, MK11 3LW, UK
UKHW021655190726
13853UKWH00001B/277